My Stars Books

THE SHELF WITH BEAUTIFUL STORIES

/MyStarsBooks

/MyStarsBooks

Thank you for your recent purchase.

Positive feedback from our valued customers really helps us to continue attracting more great customers such as yourself and to improve our work.
If you wouldn't mind leaving an online review section, we would really appreciate that.

FOOTBALL
PLAYBOOK

THIS BOOK BELONGS TO:

CONTACT INFORMATION	
NAME:	
ADDRESS:	
PHONE:	

START / END
DATES

___ / ___ / ___ TO ___ / ___ / ___

CHELSEA DAVISON

FOOTBALL PLAYBOOK

1 0

2 0

3 0

4 0

5 0

1 0

2 0

3 0

4 0

5 0

FOOTBALL PLAYBOOK

FOOTBALL PLAYBOOK

1 0
2 0
3 0
4 0
5 0

1 0
2 0
3 0
4 0
5 0

FOOTBALL PLAYBOOK

FOOTBALL PLAYBOOK

10
20
30
40
50

10
20
30
40
50

FOOTBALL PLAYBOOK

FOOTBALL PLAYBOOK

0 1
0 2
0 3
0 4
0 5

1
2
3
4
5

FOOTBALL PLAYBOOK

O 1

O 2

O 3

O 4

O 5

1 0

2 O

3 O

4 O

5 0

FOOTBALL PLAYBOOK

1
2
3
4
5

0
0
0
0
0

1
2
3
4
5

0
0
0
0
0

FOOTBALL PLAYBOOK

FOOTBALL PLAYBOOK

1
0

2
0

3
0

4
0

5
0

1
0

2
0

3
0

4
0

5
0

FOOTBALL PLAYBOOK

FOOTBALL PLAYBOOK

FOOTBALL PLAYBOOK

1
2
3
4
5

1
2
3
4
5
0

0
0
0
0
0

0
0
0
0

FOOTBALL PLAYBOOK

FOOTBALL PLAYBOOK

FOOTBALL PLAYBOOK

FOOTBALL PLAYBOOK

1 0
2 0
3 0
4 0
5 0

0 1
0 2
0 3
0 4
0 5

FOOTBALL PLAYBOOK

1 0

2 0

3 0

4 0

5 0

0 1

0 2

0 3

0 4

0 5

0 1 2 3 4 5

0 1 0 2 0 3 0 4 0 5 0

FOOTBALL PLAYBOOK

1 0

2 0

3 0

4 0

5 0

0 1

0 2

0 3

0 4

0 5

FOOTBALL PLAYBOOK

FOOTBALL PLAYBOOK

1 0

2 0

3 0

4 0

5 0

0 1

0 2

0 3

0 4

0 5

FOOTBALL PLAYBOOK

FOOTBALL PLAYBOOK

FOOTBALL PLAYBOOK

FOOTBALL PLAYBOOK

FOOTBALL PLAYBOOK

FOOTBALL PLAYBOOK

FOOTBALL PLAYBOOK

0 1
0 2
0 3
0 4
0 5

1 0
2 0
3 0
4 0
5 0

FOOTBALL PLAYBOOK

FOOTBALL PLAYBOOK

FOOTBALL PLAYBOOK

1
2
3
4
5

0
1
2
3
4
5
0

FOOTBALL PLAYBOOK

FOOTBALL PLAYBOOK

1 0

2 0

3 0

4 0

5 0

0 1

0 2

0 3

0 4

0 5

FOOTBALL PLAYBOOK

FOOTBALL PLAYBOOK

FOOTBALL PLAYBOOK

1 0

2 0

3 0

4 0

5 0

0 1

0 2

0 3

0 4

0 5

FOOTBALL PLAYBOOK

1 0
2 0
3 0
4 0
5 0

0 1
0 2
0 3
0 4
0 5

FOOTBALL PLAYBOOK

FOOTBALL PLAYBOOK

1 0
2 0
3 0
4 0
5 0

0 1
0 2
0 3
0 4
0 5 0

FOOTBALL PLAYBOOK

FOOTBALL PLAYBOOK

FOOTBALL PLAYBOOK

FOOTBALL PLAYBOOK

O 1
O 2
O 3
O 4
O 5

1 0
2 O
3 O
4 O
5 0

FOOTBALL PLAYBOOK

FOOTBALL PLAYBOOK

1 0

2 0

3 0

4 0

5 0

0 1

0 2

0 3

0 4

0 5

FOOTBALL PLAYBOOK

FOOTBALL PLAYBOOK

FOOTBALL PLAYBOOK

FOOTBALL PLAYBOOK

1 0

2 0

3 0

4 0

5 0

0 1

0 2

0 3

0 4

0 5

FOOTBALL PLAYBOOK

1 0

2 0

3 0

4 0

5 0

1 0

2 0

3 0

4 0

5 0

FOOTBALL PLAYBOOK

FOOTBALL PLAYBOOK

FOOTBALL PLAYBOOK

1 0   0 1
2 0   0 2
3 0   0 3
4 0   0 4
5 0   0 5

FOOTBALL PLAYBOOK

FOOTBALL PLAYBOOK

O 1

O 2

O 3

O 4

O 5

1 0
O

2 O

3 O

4 O

5 0

FOOTBALL PLAYBOOK

FOOTBALL PLAYBOOK

FOOTBALL PLAYBOOK

1

2

3

4

5

0

0

0

0

0

1

2

3

4

5

FOOTBALL PLAYBOOK

O 1
O 2
O 3
O 4
O 5

1 O
2 O
3 O
4 O
5 O

FOOTBALL PLAYBOOK

FOOTBALL PLAYBOOK

1   O   1   O

2   O   2   O

3   O   3   O

4   O   4   O

5   O   5

FOOTBALL PLAYBOOK

FOOTBALL PLAYBOOK

FOOTBALL PLAYBOOK

FOOTBALL PLAYBOOK

O 1

O 2

O 3

O 4

O 5

0 1

0 2

0 3

0 4

0 5

FOOTBALL PLAYBOOK

1 0
2 0
3 0
4 0
5 0

1 0
2 0
3 0
4 0
5 0

FOOTBALL PLAYBOOK

FOOTBALL PLAYBOOK

1 0
2 0
3 0
4 0
5 0

1 0
2 0
3 0
4 0
5 0

1 0

2 0

3 0

4 0

5 0

0 1

0 2

0 3

0 4

0 5

FOOTBALL PLAYBOOK

FOOTBALL PLAYBOOK

FOOTBALL PLAYBOOK

FOOTBALL PLAYBOOK

1 0

2 0

3 0

4 0

5 0

0 1

0 2

0 3

0 4

0 5

FOOTBALL PLAYBOOK

FOOTBALL PLAYBOOK

1 0
2 0
3 0
4 0
5 0

0 1
0 2
0 3
0 4
0 5

0 1 2 3 4 5

0 1 0 2 0 3 0 4 0 5 0

FOOTBALL PLAYBOOK

1 O

2 O

3 O

4 O

5 O

0 1

0 2

0 3

0 4

0 5 0

FOOTBALL PLAYBOOK

FOOTBALL PLAYBOOK

FOOTBALL PLAYBOOK

1 2 3 4 5

1 0 2 0 3 0 4 0 5 0

FOOTBALL PLAYBOOK

1 2 3 4 5

1 2 3 4 5

10
20
30
40
50

FOOTBALL PLAYBOOK

FOOTBALL PLAYBOOK

FOOTBALL PLAYBOOK

1 0

2 0

3 0

4 0

5 0

0 1

0 2

0 3

0 4

0 5

FOOTBALL PLAYBOOK

1 0

2 0

3 0

4 0

5 0

FOOTBALL PLAYBOOK

FOOTBALL PLAYBOOK

FOOTBALL PLAYBOOK

1
0

2

3

4

5

1
0

2
0

3
0

4
0

5
0

TOUCHDOWN

—

-10-   -10-

-20-   -20-

-30-   -30-

-40-   -40-

-50-   -50-

40-   -40-

30-   -30-

20-   -20-

10-   -10-

—

TOUCHDOWN

TOUCHDOWN

		-10-	-10-		
		-20	20-		
		-30	30-		
		-40	40-		
		-50	-50		
		40-	-40		
		30-	-30		
		20-	-20		
		10-	-10		

TOUCHDOWN

TOUCHDOWN

—

-10-   -10-

-20-   -20-

-30-   -30-

-40-   -40-

-50-   -50-

40-   -40-

30-   -30-

20-   -20-

10-   -10-

—

TOUCHDOWN

TOUCHDOWN

	—	
-10		10-
-20		20-
-30		30-
-40		40-
-50		50-
40-		-40
30-		-30
20-		-20
10-		-10
	—	

TOUCHDOWN

TOUCHDOWN

—

-10-   -10-

-20-   -20-

-30-   -30-

-40-   -40-

-50-   -50-

40-   -40-

30-   -30-

20-   -20-

10-   -10-

—

TOUCHDOWN

TOUCHDOWN

—

-10-   -10-

-20-   -20-

-30-   -30-

-40-   -40-

-50-   -50-

40-   -40-

30-   -30-

20-   -20-

10-   -10-

—

TOUCHDOWN

TOUCHDOWN

10
20
30
40
50
40
30
20
10

TOUCHDOWN

TOUCHDOWN

-10- / -10-

-20- / -20-

-30- / -30-

-40- / -40-

-50- / -50-

40- / -40-

30- / -30-

20- / -20-

10- / -10-

TOUCHDOWN

TOUCHDOWN

—

-10- -10-

-20- -20-

-30- -30-

-40- -40-

-50- -50-

40- -40-

30- -30-

20- -20-

10- -10-

—

TOUCHDOWN

TOUCHDOWN

—

-10-   -10-

-20-   -20-

-30-   -30-

-40-   -40-

-50-   -50-

40-   -40-

30-   -30-

20-   -20-

10-   -10-

—

TOUCHDOWN

TOUCHDOWN

—

-10- 10-

-20- 20-

-30- 30-

-40- 40-

-50- -50-

40- -40-

30- -30-

20- -20-

10- -10-

—

TOUCHDOWN

TOUCHDOWN

—

-10- | -10-
-20- | -20-
-30- | -30-
-40- | -40-
-50- | -50-
40- | -40
30- | -30
20- | -20
10- | -10

—

TOUCHDOWN

TOUCHDOWN

—

-10- -10-

-20- -20-

-30- -30-

-40- -40-

-50- -50-

40- -40-

30- -30-

20- -20-

10- -10-

—

TOUCHDOWN

TOUCHDOWN

	—	
-10-		-10-
-20-		-20-
-30-		-30-
-40-		-40-
-50-		-50-
-40-		-40-
-30-		-30-
-20-		-20-
-10-		-10-
	—	

TOUCHDOWN

TOUCHDOWN

	—	
-10-		-10-
-20-		-20-
-30-		-30-
-40-		-40-
-50-		-50-
-40-		-40-
-30-		-30-
-20-		-20-
-10-		-10-
	—	

TOUCHDOWN

TOUCHDOWN

—

-10- 10-

-20- 20-

-30- 30-

-40- 40-

-50- -50-

40- -40-

30- -30-

20- -20-

10- -10-

—

TOUCHDOWN

TOUCHDOWN

—

-10- 10-

-20- 20-

-30- 30-

-40- 40-

-50- 50-

40- -40-

30- -30-

20- -20-

10- -10-

—

TOUCHDOWN

TOUCHDOWN

—10	I	10—
—20		20—
—30		30—
—40		40—
—50		—50
40—		—40
30—		—30
20—		—20
10—	I	—10

TOUCHDOWN

TOUCHDOWN

—

-10-   -10-

-20-   -20-

-30-   -30-

-40-   -40-

-50-   -50-

40-   -40-

30-   -30-

20-   -20-

10-   -10-

—

TOUCHDOWN

TOUCHDOWN

	—	
-10		-10
-20		-20
-30		-30
-40		-40
-50		-50
40-		-40
30-		-30
20-		-20
10-		-10
	—	

TOUCHDOWN

TOUCHDOWN

—

-10-   -10-
-20-   -20-
-30-   -30-
-40-   -40-
-50-   -50-
-40-   -40-
-30-   -30-
-20-   -20-
-10-   -10-

—

TOUCHDOWN

TOUCHDOWN

—

-10 · 10-

-20 · 20-

-30 · 30-

-40 · 40-

-50 · -50

40- · -40

30- · -30

20- · -20

10- · -10

—

TOUCHDOWN

TOUCHDOWN

—

-10-   10-

-20-   20-

-30-   30-

-40-   40-

-50-   -50-

40-   -40-

30-   -30-

20-   -20-

10-   -10-

—

TOUCHDOWN